I Belong In Music

Written by
Dr. Arnekua Jackson

Illustrated by
C.J. Love

Published by: Dr. Arnekua Jackson
Contact Info: IBelongInMusic@gmail.com

Printed in the United States of America

Dedication:

-To God, my family, Princess Davis (editor and dear friend), and my music professors who have inspired me tremendously:
Dr. Kimberly VanWeelden, Dr. Charlie J. Toomer, and Dr. Luvada Harrison.

-To my music students: Dream Big! You are true game-changers.
Continue making music and if you can't find a space in it, create one.

-And to my fellow music educators, keep inspiring and know your work is not in vain.

Before I go to bed, I sit up and watch the cars go by...

Daydreaming about the music that keeps me from being shy.

2

3

My toes keep tapping, my feet are stamping, I'm dancing everywhere!
I can't stop the music in my head, and nothing can compare.

4

When morning comes, I brush my teeth and hurry to get dressed.

I rush to Ms. Jordan's music class because I'm always so impressed.

5

Ms. Jordan is my favorite teacher who has such big, thick hair.

I can't help to feel the joy she brings that always fills the air.

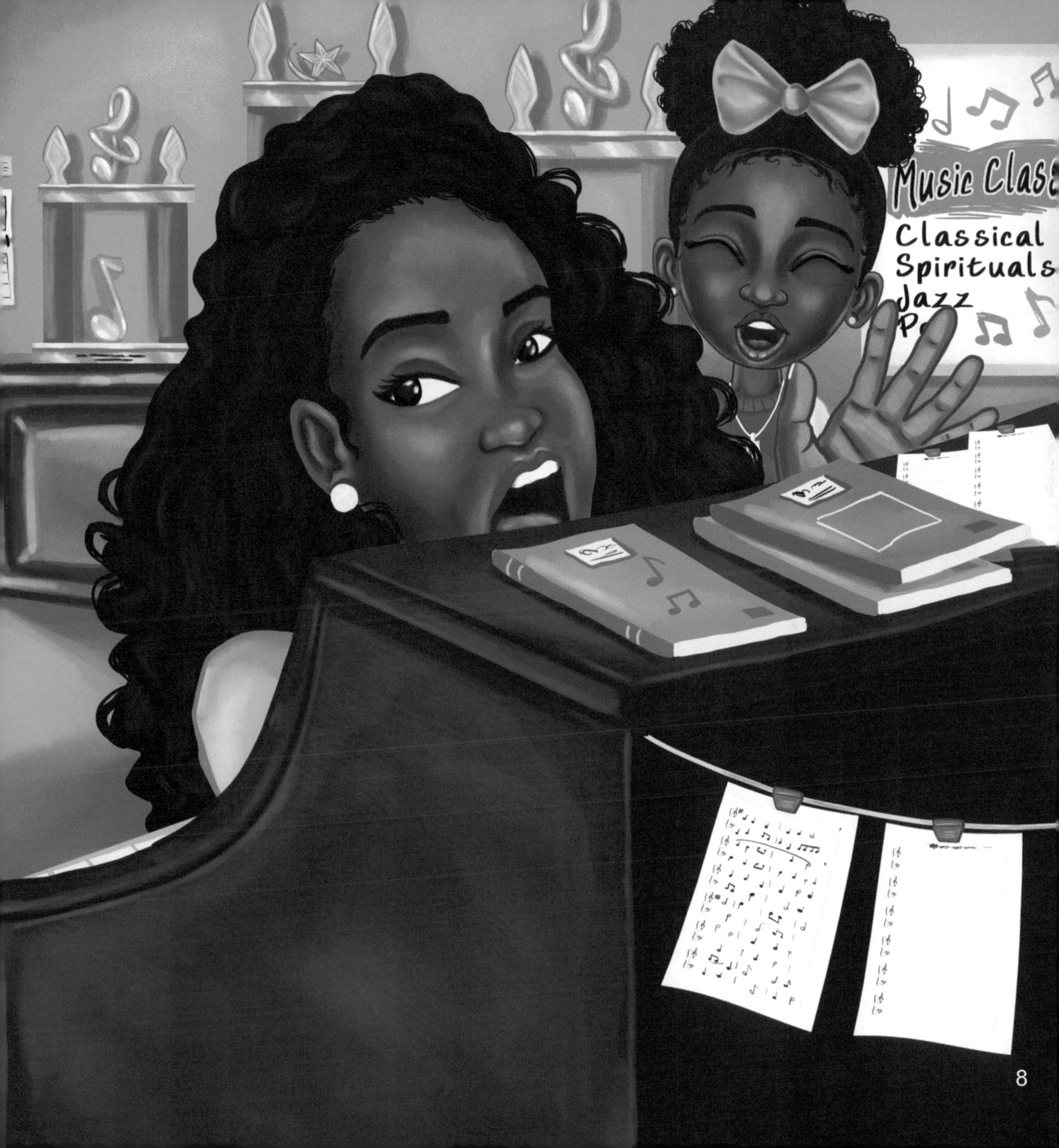
Music Clas
Classical
Spirituals
Jazz

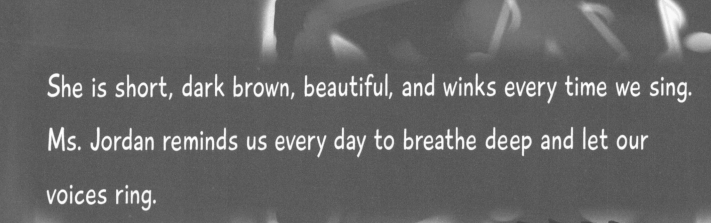

She is short, dark brown, beautiful, and winks every time we sing.
Ms. Jordan reminds us every day to breathe deep and let our
voices ring.

I love my music class because we all feel like we belong.

There is nothing we can't do because she always picks the perfect song.

Classical, Spirituals, Jazz, and Pop are just to name a few.

We perform these music genres to show what we can do.

14

When I grow up, I want to be just like Ms. Jordan-
A beautiful woman who soars in music.

16

She looks like me, sounds like me, and makes me feel so free. When I sing, I know I belong because of the music Ms. Jordan instilled in me.

CHOIR DISPLAY

18

I Belong to Music

Story by Arnekua Jackson

Music & Lyrics by Samantha Minor

19

Some - times, you might, be the on - ly one__ in a big, filled up room,__ who looks like you do.__ But it does - n't take much, to make you feel free,__ just a friend with a tune.__ When they sing it for you,__ you'll see,__ you be-lo - ng to mu - sic.__ There's just,__ so much,__ you will get__ to learn,__

all the rhy - thms and mel - o - dies,_ for eve-ry - one and eve-ry_

_ bo - dy. And in a_ sec - ond,_ you will start to feel,_

_ the way mu - sic loves,_ and the way mu - sic heals._ To - day,_

you'll say,_ I be-long to mu - sic, and

4

it be-longs to me,_____ 'cause when it comes to mu - sic, there's no-thing I_____ can't be. Mu - sic does-n't mind_____ if you feel diff-erent, or_____ just left be-hind.. There's a song for eve - ry-thing, and it's al-ways just_ the one_____ you need.

I Belong to Music

INTRO
Bb   F/A   Gm   Eb

CHORUS
Bb
I belong to music
   F/A
And it belongs to me
    Gm
'Cause when it comes to music
    Eb
There's nothing I can't be
Bb
Music doesn't mind
    F/A
If you feel different or just left behind
Gm
There's a song for everything,
    Eb
And it's always just the one you need

INTERLUDE
Bb   F/A

VERSE 1
Bb
Sometimes you might
  F/A
Be the only one
   Eb
In a big, filled up room
    Eb
Who looks like you do
   Bb
But it doesn't take much
  F/A
To make you feel free
   Eb
Just a friend with a tune
    Eb
When they sing it for you
   F   Eb
You'll see, you belong to music

VERSE 2
Bb
There's just, so much,
F/A
You will get to learn
    Eb
All the rhythms and melodies
    Eb
For everyone and everybody
   Bb
And in a second,
F/A
You will start to feel
   Eb
They way music lvoves
   Eb
The way music heals
  F   Eb
Today, you'll say

CHORUS
Bb
I belong to music
   F/A
And it belongs to me
    Gm
'Cause when it comes to music
    Eb
There's nothing I can't be
Bb
Music doesn't mind
    F/A
If you feel different or just left behind
Gm
There's a song for everything,
    Eb
And it's always just the one you need

OUTRO
Bb   F/A   Gm   Eb

23

About the Author

Dr. Arnekua Jackson is a dream maker, culture disrupter, and an award-winning choral director and music educator that has served grades K through 12 for over ten years. She graduated with a Bachelor's of Music Education degree from Florida Agricultural and Mechanical University. She received both her Master's of Music Education and Doctor of Philosophy in Music Education from Florida State University.

As a Title 1, elementary level teacher, Dr. Jackson has spent most of her career teaching General Music and building a choral program implementing instructional strategies that support core content growth. As a high school choral director, she continues this practice with enthusiasm and passion for helping students identify and enrich their musical talents. While serving in these teaching roles, Dr. Jackson has earned Teacher of the Year, Distinguished Educator of the Year, was awarded two Mayoral Proclamations, and received many more accolades.

Dr. Jackson noticed the lack of minority children's literature available to teachers and students in the music classroom. Birthed out of her desire to promote the importance of cultural representations, Dr. Jackson endeavors to increase the visibility of positive minority characters, text themes, and illustrations that inspire children to be life-long musicians.

In her spare time, Dr. Jackson presents at state and national conferences for music education, enjoys traveling around the world, mentoring minority girls, and developing music research that promotes transcultural learning and diversity in the field.

Dr. Jackson currently resides in her hometown Boynton Beach, Florida.

This is her debut children's book.

Illustrated & Designed By:

C.J. Love

C.love2design@gmail.com

www.clove2design.com